## Books by Dorothy Sterling

BILLY GOES EXPLORING

BROWNIE SCOUT MYSTERY

CAPTAIN OF THE PLANTER,
  The Story of Robert Smalls

THE CUB SCOUT MYSTERY

FREEDOM TRAIN,
  The Story of Harriet Tubman

INSECTS AND THE HOMES THEY BUILD

MARY JANE

POLIO PIONEERS

THE SILVER SPOON MYSTERY

SOPHIE AND HER PUPPIES

THE STORY OF MOSSES, FERNS, AND MUSHROOMS

TREES AND THEIR STORY

UNITED NATIONS, N.Y.

WALL STREET,
  The Story of the Stock Market

## Illustrated by Winifred Lubell

CREATURES OF THE NIGHT

THE STORY OF CAVES

CREATURES OF THE NIGHT

# CREATURES
# OF
# THE NIGHT

by Dorothy Sterling
illustrated by Winifred Lubell

DOUBLEDAY & COMPANY, INC., GARDEN CITY, NEW YORK

# Contents

# CREATURES OF THE NIGHT

## Chapter One

### FACES AT THE WINDOW

The sun slowly sinks behind the treetops. Shadows lengthen, spread, deepen. The first star shines in a darkening sky. On his perch in the oak tree, a sleepy robin tucks his head under his wing.

Good morning. It's time to wake up!

As if on signal from the setting sun, a hundred, a thousand, a million creatures begin to stir.

What kind of topsy-turvy world is this? What's the idea of getting up when the sun is going down?

It's not topsy-turvy at all. *You* live on the day shift, along with green plants that need the energy of the sun to make food. You follow the timetable of the butterflies and bees, the chittering squirrels and the chattering monkeys. But most of the members of the animal kingdom have a different schedule. Your evening is their morning.

The world of the night is the world of the deer and the mouse, the timid rabbit and the sharp-nosed fox, skunk, raccoon, 'possum, and blinking owl. It's also the world of a host of smaller creatures.

As the sky darkens, these creatures crawl from under stones, clamber up grass blades, take off from tree-trunk runways to spread their wings in the still air. They hunt and eat, mate and raise their families. When the stars grow pale and the robin wakes to sing his early-morning song to the sun, then, like a million Cinderellas leaving a million balls, they scurry back to their homes and hiding places.

The Late Show that they put on is like nothing you have ever seen before. From opening night in spring until the first frosts of fall, they perform on your lawn and in your garden. There's a buzz, a whir of wings as their orchestra tunes up. Some of the actors assemble at your window every summer evening.

Beauty queens, warriors, acrobats, a fat comedian, and a famous fiddler——

"But"—you sound disappointed—"they're just bugs."

Just bugs, indeed! Why, that lovely green creature with the golden eyes is the mother of a lion. Her yellow-winged neighbor used to be a bear. The awkward fellow who's banging against the glass is first cousin to an ancient Egyp-

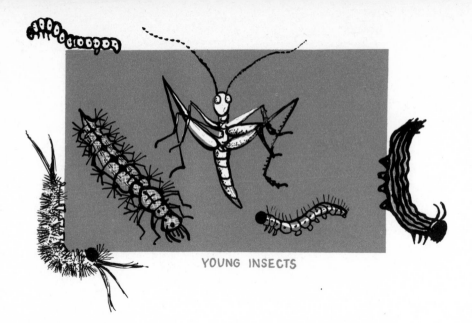

YOUNG INSECTS

eyed Lacewing is a dragonlike creature with ferocious curving jaws. Caterpillars, large and small, naked and hairy, are crawling over the glass. Only the Katydid, the long-legged music-maker, is still recognizable.

Almost all of these insect infants—grub, dragon, cater-pillar—grow up in the same way. The Luna Moth who is slowly opening and closing her graceful wings started life last summer as a tiny green caterpillar. Wingless, worm-like, she knew only one commandment: EAT! She ate and grew and shed her skin until she was twenty times as big as when she hatched from an egg. Then she stopped eating and spun a cocoon.

All winter long she rested inside her silken home. All winter long her caterpillar body slowly changed. This morning, at last, the changes were complete and she crawled from the cocoon with the pale green wings, velvet legs, and feathery antennae of a moth.

Now she is ready to obey the second law of the insect world: PROVIDE FOR A FAMILY.

Tonight she will mate. Tomorrow night she will fly through the woods, fastening her eggs to the leaves of walnut and hickory trees. A night later, two nights later, she will die.

This complicated way of growing up is known as *metamorphosis*, from a Greek word meaning "change shape." The hungry insect baby—whether it is a Luna caterpillar or a beetle grub—is called a *larva*. The resting, changing 'tween-ager is a *pupa* (pronounced pew-pa). The full-grown winged insect is an *adult*. Some kinds of insects need only a week or two to become full-grown. For others the metamorphosis takes three years.

Katydids, and their cousins the crickets and grasshoppers, have an *incomplete metamorphosis*. Their babies, called *nymphs*, are small, wingless copies of the adult insects. The grow and shed their skins until at last their wings appear. After that, they settle down to the business of mating and egg laying.

Insects invented metamorphosis two hundred twenty million years ago when the warm moist air of the ancient coal forests gave way to glacial cold. All of the animals living then had to find ways to make the best of a brief summer and a short-lived food supply—or become extinct.

Some met the challenge by growing smaller. Others experimented. They became feeding machines as children and egg-laying machines when adult, with a resting period in-between which tided them over long winters or seasons of drought. This triple life was so successful that by the time the pterodactyl was gliding through the air on its leathery wings, it had thousands of different kinds of insects for company.

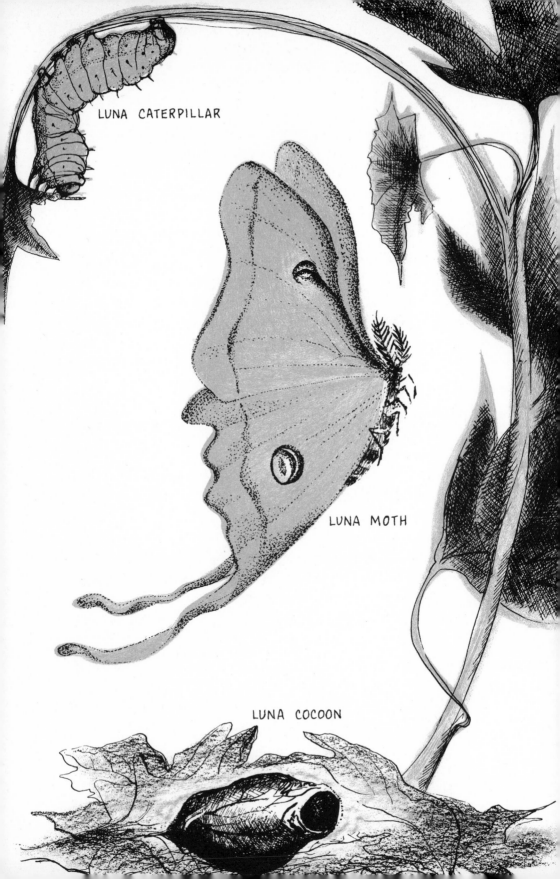

LUNA CATERPILLAR

LUNA MOTH

LUNA COCOON

## When Is a Bug Not a Bug?

Perhaps it's time to stop talking about metamorphosis and pterodactyls and come back to a three-letter word.

When is a bug not a bug?

When it's a beetle, of course. Or a moth. Or a cricket.

This isn't a riddle or a joke. A bug is a very special kind of insect with four wings and a jointed beak through which it sucks its food. A June-bug is NOT a bug. A lady-bug is NOT a bug. Neither is a caterpillar or a mosquito or a fly.

To call every one of these different creatures a bug is like calling every flower a rose or every tree a maple. Or every boy, John. You can't do anything about insects—raise them, collect them, or even exterminate them—without knowing something about them. Without first sorting them out and grouping them together in some fashion.

Two hundred years ago, Karl von Linné, a Swedish scientist, worked out a way to classify all animals and plants. Instead of lumping together the green insects and the blue flowers and the birds-who-live-in-oak-trees, he grouped them according to the structure of their bodies.

He started out by asking questions. Does an insect have two wings or four? Are these wings hard or soft, covered with scales or transparent? Is its mouth intended for biting or for sucking?

He counted wings and studied mouth parts with a magnifying glass until he had arranged the entire insect army into tidy brigades and regiments. Because the language of educated people of his time was Latin, he gave Latin names to the divisions, rather than English or Swedish ones. He even changed his own name to Carolus Linnaeus.

According to his plan, insects are grouped in two dozen

or so different *orders*. (There is a list of the most important orders on p. 120.) Butterflies and moths which have two pairs of scale-covered wings are in one order. Beetles, whose outer wings are hard and shell-like, make up another order, and those pesky two-winged creatures, the flies and mosquitoes, a third. Katydids and grasshoppers are grouped together and there's a separate order for bugs.

Within each order, insects who are closely related to each other are grouped in *families*. You probably call the noisy creature who's banging on your window a June-bug. Actually, it's a beetle and a member of the ancient and honorable family of Scarab Beetles. Since there are 30,000 different kinds of Scarabs in the world, the family is further divided into *genera* (*genus* is the singular) and the genera into *species*. If you want to be formal in the way you address your June-bug, you must say that it is a member of the order *Coleoptera* (see pronunciation on p. 120), that its family name is *Scarabaeidae*, its genus *Phyllophaga*, and its species *fusca*. Or just *Phyllophaga fusca* for short!

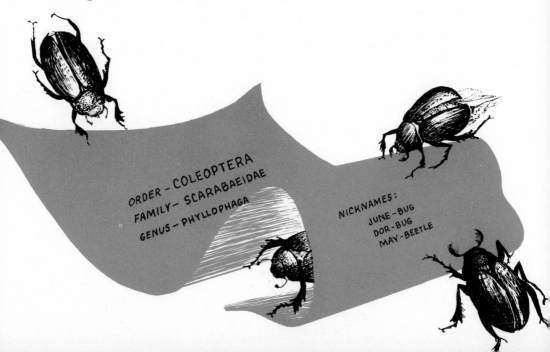

ORDER – COLEOPTERA
FAMILY – SCARABAEIDAE
GENUS – PHYLLOPHAGA

NICKNAMES:
JUNE-BUG
DOR-BUG
MAY-BEETLE

"What's the point of these orders and families, these tongue-twisting Latin names?" you groan.

The point is to avoid confusion. The point is to know EXACTLY which insect you are talking about and who its close relatives are.

For instance, a June-bug is sometimes called a May-beetle, sometimes a Dor-bug. But in England a Dor-bug is a different beetle entirely, different in shape, in size, and in feeding habits. If you were going to discuss Dor-bugs with a pen pal in London or read up on them in a British book, you would have to use their scientific name.

For instance, a firefly isn't a fly, nor is a lightning-bug a bug or a glowworm a worm. Instead all three are one and the same small beetle. And how are you going to talk about the Dobsonfly who is neither fly or bug, although it is called Conniption-Bug, Hellgrammite, and Water-grampus?

Actually, you don't need to worry about learning names like *Coleoptera* and *Phyllophaga* right now. Even the entomologists, the scientists who specialize in studying insects, don't know the names of all of the insects in the world, or even in the United States. There are too many.

For this summer the important thing to remember is that insects are not "just bugs." The brigades and regiments, the orders and families, are alike in many ways and different in others. A caterpillar will never grow up to be a beetle. A beetle will never sing like a cricket. A cricket will never fly like a moth or sting like a mosquito or light up like a firefly. The important thing to remember is that a bug is a bug and NOT a beetle or a moth or a cricket.

# Chapter Two

## BRIGHT LIGHTS AT NIGHT

ACT ONE

*Scene: A window in the suburbs*

*Time: An evening in late spring*

*A moth flies on stage. Circling around hesitantly, it rests on the window only to back off again. Beating its wings, it flies to the top of the pane, darts away, flutters back. Slender legs cling to the glass. Wings make a faint sound as they open, close, open.*

*A second moth flies in and a third. Each flutters about, hesitates, then lands and spreads its wings.*

*All is quiet until—brzz—buzz—bang! Enter the June-bug. Noisily it flaps about. Clumsily it batters its plump body against the glass.*

You switch off the television set and walk to the window. The moths are motionless, facing the living-room light. The beetle is bumping about, as if it were a child having a tantrum.

Why have these insects come here? Why aren't they flying in the yard, eating their supper, and minding their own business? Why are they trying to come into the house?

"Go 'way," you tell them, hitting against the glass.

Startled, the insects take off, only to return a moment later. You try it again and again, but it's no use. You can't chase them away. Even if you go outside and catch them, they make little attempt to escape. It's as if they were drawn to the window by a magnet, as if they were under a spell.

## Song of the Light

The truth is, they are under a spell. Do you remember the story of the Sirens, a trio of sweet-singing sea nymphs who lived on a rocky island? Sailors couldn't resist following the Sirens' song, although it meant shipwreck and death.

The light in your living room is the insects' siren. They MUST fly toward it. Even if they are hungry. Even if the light is an open flame which will destroy them.

The Sirens of old met their match in Ulysses when he was returning home from the Trojan War. As he drew near the fateful island he plugged the ears of his crew with wax and ordered himself tied to the mast. Although he heard the sweet music, he couldn't escape from his bonds to follow it.

Ulysses was able to save himself because he thought and planned ahead. This is something that the insects on your window cannot do. Remarkable as they are, they are creatures of little brain. When the light calls, they automatically answer.

It's not a question of obeying, as you obey your mother. It's a mechanical, unthinking obedience. They have no more choice in the matter than a needle does when a magnet pulls it.

Like a magnet, the pull of the light is an actual physical force. Scientists studying it have named it *phototropism*, a word which means "turning toward the light." The same word is used in describing plants which also move toward light, lengthening their stems and twisting their leaves to follow it.

Not all night insects fall under the spell of light. Some are *negatively phototropic*, which means that they skitter AWAY from light as fast as they can go. Clothes moths and cockroaches behave like this as you will see in chapters three and six. Other insects follow different pulls at different times of their lives. Sometimes it is not light but smell which attracts them. When a male Luna Moth crawls from his cocoon, he MUST respond to the odor of a female Luna. He will travel for miles through bramble thickets or along city streets, facing unbelievable hardships and dangers, until he has found and mated with a female moth.

Although scientists have names for these siren calls they don't know exactly how they work. Their guess is that the pull is a chemical one, that light (or odor) reacts on substances in the insect's body. No one has ever seen these substances, even under a powerful microscope, but perhaps that is because they haven't looked hard enough yet.

### "Bug Bulbs"

Even though the mystery of phototropism is still unsolved, new facts about it are being discovered all the time. Not long ago, scientists at the General Electric Company set up an outdoor laboratory. They built nine traps in which to catch insects. Each trap was lit by a bulb of a different color. With colors ranging from red through yellow and green to blue and violet, their experiment looked like a rainbow.

Every night they turned on the lights. Every morning they counted their catch. It didn't take long to discover that most night insects don't see red at all. There were scarcely any insects in the red-lighted trap while those at the other end of the rainbow—the blue and violet ones— had plenty of customers. And the ultraviolet lamp whose light is invisible to human eyes did the best business of all.

Perhaps you're wondering why they bothered to do this. Aside from a handful of insect collectors, who cares what color light moths and beetles prefer?

The man on the night shift at a brightly lit airport cares. So does the owner of a drive-in movie or a frozen-custard stand—and even the cook at your own back-yard grill. Everyone who works outdoors on a summer night cares. Because they want lights which will keep insects AWAY.

The farmer cares, too, for a different reason. He's carrying on a battle against the corn borers, the codling moths, the tobacco worms which eat his crops. For him, light can be a weapon in this everlasting war. He wants a light which will bring insects TO him, a light which will lead them to traps, so that they can be destroyed.

After the scientists' experiment, lamp manufacturers started making colored "bug bulbs" to use outdoors at night and——

"Red bulbs," you suggest, "because insects don't see red lights at all."

No, you're not quite right. Red bulbs are fine in photographic darkrooms, but have you ever tried to read under a red light? Or eat a hamburger in one's rosy glow? If so, you'll probably agree that it is neither a pleasant nor efficient light.

Instead of using red, the lamp manufacturers chose the next best color—yellow. A yellow "bug bulb" doesn't actually chase night-flying insects away, but it removes most of the blue light that attracts them.

How about the farmer who wants to trap insects? In your grandfather's day, he trapped them with a candle or a kerosene lamp. Today he hangs an elegant ultraviolet light in his field and leads the corn borers and tobacco-worm moths to their doom.

## Insect Appeal

Do you know those advertisements that begin, "You too can be tall . . . or beautiful . . . or learn to play the piano"? Well, you too can make use of the scientists' discoveries. You too can have insect appeal.

Instead of waiting for the creatures of the night to fly to your window, you can go outdoors and call them with a light. Ultraviolet lamps are expensive, but right next to the yellow "bug bulbs" on hardware store shelves you'll see blue ones. If you borrow an extension cord from your father and light one of these blue bulbs in your yard you'll be positively irresistible.

The only other equipment you'll need is an old sheet. Moths sometimes circle a light for hours on end, but beetles and other insects often drop to the ground underneath it. With the sheet spread out on the grass, you'll be able to get a good look at all of your night visitors.

As the siren call of the light travels to the far corners of your yard, insects will hurry to answer it. Different creatures will come at different times—the June-bug and Luna Moth in spring, the Lacewing and Click Beetle in summer, and the Katydid in the weeks before fall. From April to October you're sure to have company.

Some evenings, perhaps, you can visit other people's lights. Where are the biggest, brightest lights in your town? Street lamps, store windows, neon signs? The lights at the amusement park or the golf driving range? Where would you go if you were a phototropic night-flying insect?

caterpillars also live inside folded leaves, either alone or with two or three brothers for company.

Another small moth who will probably visit your light late in summer is the Goldenrod Gall Moth. This gray-brown moth is best known for its unusual home. The story of the home starts in spring when the moth lays her eggs on goldenrod plants. After the caterpillars hatch, they eat their way into the stems of the goldenrod.

GALL

While the caterpillar feeds and grows, the plant grows, too. Only instead of growing in a normal way, the golden-rod surrounds its guest with an odd, spindle-shaped bulge. The caterpillar hasn't built this guest room. The bulge, known as a *gall*, is the work of the goldenrod.

Before the caterpillar changes into a pupa, it chews a hole near the top of the gall and closes the opening with a silken plug. Can you guess what this is for? It's a door-way—an exit—for the moth-to-be whose mouth won't be built for chewing. A month later, when the moth is ready to fly, it pushes out the plug and takes off.

If you poke around among the goldenrod in your neigh-borhood, looking two thirds of the way up their stems, you won't have much difficulty finding one of these galls. Perhaps the caterpillar will be at home to greet you. If so, you must be sure to bow and address it by its scientific name: *Gnorimoschema gallaesolidaginis*. Its name is longer than its wormlike body!

Some of the moths resting on your sheet are even smaller than the Goldenrod Gall Moth or the Close-Wings or Plume. These are Leaf-miners. That is, their caterpil-

35

PLUME MOTH

lars live inside leaves. Not rolled up in a leaf or resting on one, but actually INSIDE, between the leaf's upper and lower surfaces. As the caterpillar feeds, it mines through the leaf's tissue, leaving a winding trail which can be seen from the outside. People sometimes call these pale trails on leaves "spirit writing." (Moth caterpillars are not the only spirit writers. There's also a family of tiny flies that like to practice penmanship.)

If you bring home a Leaf-miner Moth, you may hear an objection from your mother. That's because it looks so much like its cousin, the unpopular Clothes Moth. The Clothes Moth larva is one of the few caterpillars who is not a vegetarian. Spurning juicy, vitamin-rich green leaves, it prefers instead to feast on your newest lamb's-wool sweater.

Even though the Leaf-miner and Clothes Moth look alike, you'll have no trouble in telling them apart, because the Clothes Moth hates light. It will always fly AWAY from light to the darkest part of a room. You can impress your mother by explaining that it is negatively photo-tropic!

LEAF-MINER MOTH

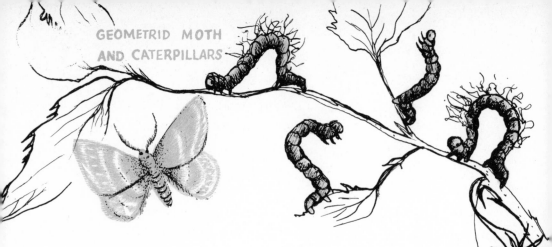

## Rainbow Pebbles

The micro-moths are gray, silver, tan, the patterns on their wings difficult to see without a magnifying glass. But many of the middle-sized moths are gaily colored. There's an old Indian legend which explains their origins.

Long, long ago when the Great Spirit was putting the world together, he wanted people to love nature and seek out its beauties. After he'd raised the mountains and scooped out the valleys, he heaped up piles of wonderfully colored pebbles. Then he called in the South Wind and commanded it to blow life into the pebbles. As the wind blew, the pebbles rose and flew away, their wings the colors of the rainbow.

One flying pebble that you're almost sure to see is the Geometrid Moth. Leaf green, with wavy white lines decorating its wings, it's as pretty as its caterpillar is funny-looking.

Most caterpillars are well-supplied with feet. They have six forelegs and ten stubby *prolegs* which grow from their abdomens. The Geometrid caterpillars, however, have only four prolegs. They hump along, looping their bodies upward, then flattening them out again. Because of

37

this peculiar walking style, they're known as Measuring-worms—or Inch-worms—or Loopers.

Another family of brightly colored moths are the Slug Moths. Green and cinnamon-brown, red-brown and white, the adults will often come to your light. It's their caterpillars, however, that you're most likely to remember. Their forelegs are tiny and they haven't any prolegs at all. They don't crawl or hump along. They flow. When they glide across a leaf, they move like tiny tanks.

There are dozens of other attractive moths who fly to lights. At least once during the summer you'll probably see the Rosy Maple Moth, a dainty creature with pink and pale yellow wings. Or the black and white Leopard Moth, a member of the Carpenter Moth family whose larvae bore into the trunks of trees. But the prize catch of them all, the biggest and most breathtakingly beautiful, are the Saturnids, better known as Giant Silkworm Moths.

LEOPARD
MOTH

### Giants

They truly are giants. The Cecropia's velvet wings are almost as wide as this page and the Polyphemus and Luna are only slightly smaller. Even their caterpillars are the biggest things in the caterpillar line—fat, sausage-shaped creatures longer than your middle finger.

They truly are silkworms. Their larvae spin big cocoons of tough waterproof silk. The Polyphemus's cocoon is formed of one unbroken silk thread, eight hundred feet long. It would be quite possible to weave this thread into cloth.

SLUG MOTH AND
CATERPILLAR

Store-bought silk, the kind actually used for dresses and ties, is manufactured by an Asian relative of the Saturnids. Many people have tried to raise these caterpillars in this country, including Benjamin Franklin who ran a silkworm plantation in Pennsylvania before the Revolution. All of these attempts failed because of the enormous amount of patience and hand labor required. Even if they had been successful, however, you would never find the Asian moth fluttering around your light. It has been tamed for so long that it has lost the ability to fly.

Although American Silk Moths fly to lights, each species operates on a different time schedule. The Promethea flits about at dusk and in the early evening. The Luna waits for its namesake, the moon, and the Cecropia usually remains hidden until long past your bedtime.

Because of this, the surest way of making the acquaintance of most of these giants is to raise them from cocoons. When the trees are bare in winter, you'll see gray silk cocoons fastened to twigs or resting on the ground, partly covered by fallen leaves. Even in the city there are cocoons to be found in the park—or for sale in butterfly supply houses. If you bring some home with you, it's best to keep them in a cool place and to sprinkle them occasionally so that they don't dry out.

Nothing will happen all winter long. Then, one fine spring morning when the leaves are coming out on the trees, you'll notice signs of life. First, a rustling noise. The cocoon wriggles and a damp spot appears at one end. The

39

softened threads bulge as the insect inside struggles to set itself free. At last the walls of silk give way and a damp, bedraggled creature crawls out. It has a furry fat body and six waving legs but where its wings ought to be there are only rumpled pads.

Slowly the moth climbs up a twig. It clings there, motionless. Slowly its wings unfold. In an hour you can see the rich red, white, and velvet brown of Cecropia or Ceanothus, the blue and gold eye spots of Polyphemus, or the trailing green tails of a Luna. Another hour and the moth is still resting on the twig, pumping its wings up and down, up and down, until they are dry.

The delicately colored antennae are almost as lovely as the wings. No other moth has feelers that are quite as fern-like and feathery. Or as big and branching. Or as sensitive.

Although the female Silk Moths are usually larger than the males, with more brightly colored wings, their antennae are smaller. There's a reason for this difference, a reason that you can observe for yourself if, among your hatching cocoons, you have a female.

Late in the afternoon on her birthday, move your lady to a screen porch or a cage next to an open window. Be sure to use wire screening rather than glass for a cage because she must be able to say "Come to me. Come to me" in the only way she knows how—through her scent.

As the sun sets and the wind dies down, she will begin to broadcast her message, sending it far and wide on the cool evening air. You can't smell her perfume, but miles away in woods or park the sensitive antennae of male moths receive the siren call and hasten to obey.

PROMETHEA MOTH

POLYPHEMUS MOTHS

It isn't long before you hear a noise, see a shadow on your screen. A giant moth, flapping his broad wings, is trying to get inside. Soon a second, a third, are fluttering about. When you open the porch door, they swoop toward the waiting female.

"Maybe it's not the lady's perfume," you object. "Maybe the males have X-ray vision or second sight. Maybe they just happened to be passing and dropped in."

For centuries, naturalists have observed and reported on the flight of male Silk Moths. Through a series of experiments, they have definitely established its cause. If the perfume-producing organ is removed from a female, the males will flutter toward the tiny fragment, paying no attention at all to the lovely living moth. They will fly over hill and dale to mate with a headless female. But if the lady is kept under glass or the male's plumelike antennae are snipped off, he won't bother to do any traveling. It isn't X-ray vision or accident—or love. It's just chemistry.

JUNE-BUGS

*Chapter Four*

## CIRCUS PARADE

*"The time has come," the Walrus said,*
*"To talk of many things:*
*Of noisy clowns and pinching bugs——*
*Of ancient gods and kings——*
*Of tumblers and of acrobats——*
*And lions who have wings."*

The time has come to talk about the circus that is parading toward your light. On any warm spring evening that fat clown, the June-bug, leads the procession. Noisily, it crashes against the bulb. Clumsily it tumbles to the sheet underneath. When you look at its stout chestnut-colored body, you wonder how it manages to fly. It doesn't even seem to have wings.

Have you ever seen a picture of a roadable plane? A flying automobile? It's an airplane with folding wings. When it lands on the highway its wings fold away and it becomes a car. Everyone agrees that it's a dandy invention —even though the June-bug thought of it first.

Along with the rest of the beetle tribe, June-bugs have

44

two pairs of wings. The top pair, which meets in a line along the middle of the insect's back, is hard and shell-like. Known as *elytra*, from a Greek word meaning "sheath," they serve as protective covering for the gauzy underwings.

When a June-bug takes off, it raises its elytra and holds them out stiffly while the underwings do the actual work of flying. When it lands, the filmy wings disappear. Like the wings of a roadable plane, they are folded neatly away under the elytra.

June-bugs have a whole bag of tricks. At night under the spell of a light, they sit with their spiny legs stretched out and their flaglike antennae held upright. During the day they hide on the ground or in clumps of grass. If they are disturbed, they fold their legs tightly against their bodies and fit their antennae into little grooves. It's a case of "Now you see them. Now you don't." By remaining perfectly still, they manage to make themselves invisible.

The Asiatic Garden Beetle, a smaller member of the Scarab family, is also an expert at playing possum. Early in summer, if you live in the East, you're likely to see half a dozen of these cinnamon-brown beetles at your light or nibbling flower petals in the garden. When you reach out to catch one, it doesn't fly. It doubles up its legs and plummets to the ground, lying motionless until you are convinced that it is dead. Only after all danger seems past will antennae poke out, legs unfold, and the beetle scurry away.

ASIATIC GARDEN BEETLE

REAL SIZE

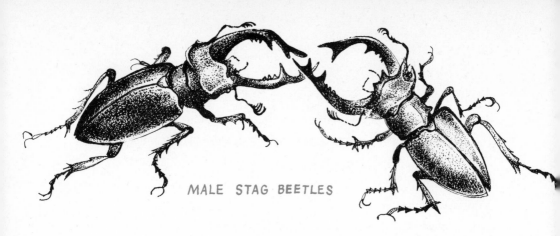

MALE STAG BEETLES

A midsummer visitor to lights, the shiny, hard-shelled Stag Beetle has a different method of defense. Male Stags are equipped with enormous pincer jaws that look like antlers. If danger threatens, they don't try to hide. Instead, they raise their heads, open their jaws, and DARE anyone to attack. They'll fight at the drop of a leaf, especially if a lady Stag is nearby.

Over the centuries, these battling beetles have captured men's imaginations. Ancient Romans hung Stag pincers around their necks to ward off sickness, while in northern Europe people called them "fire starters," believing that they carried live coals in their curving jaws. Perhaps the most famous Stag Beetle of all is the one that Tom Sawyer took to church with him. Did you ever read about Tom's pinch-bug who nipped a poodle and brought the pastor's sermon to a standstill?

## Members of the Underground

FEMALE
STAG BEETLE

Night after night you'll see beetles at your light or chewing on the leaves of trees nearby. Then, suddenly, they'll disappear. No matter how hard you look, you won't see them again. What has happened to them? Where have they gone?

REAL SIZE

tablets, people learned science the hard way—by firsthand observation. Often their observations were correct, but they drew the wrong conclusions about them.

Thousands of years ago Egyptians were fascinated by the comings and goings of a species of Scarab. Fascinated and puzzled. The beetles appeared in large numbers, only to disappear a short time later. The high priest watched them dig down into the soil and emerge from it. Knowing nothing of eggs and grubs, the observers decided that they were seeing the same insects all the time.

"They live forever," the priests concluded. "They bury themselves, then return to life. If we worship these immortal creatures we too will live forever. Even after we are dead and buried we too will return to life again."

There was lots more to it than that. Perhaps because all of the observers were men, it was decided that all of the beetles were males also, and representatives of a warrior race. Worship of the Scarab became part of the worship of Ra, god of the sun and, indeed, of all creation.

The stout shell-backed insects were embalmed, just as

the Pharaohs were. Their mummies were placed in tombs and their likenesses carved in precious stones and painted on temple walls. When an important man died, his heart was removed and a Scarab put in its place. Centuries later Roman soldiers were still wearing rings with carved images of the sacred beetle to bring them luck in battle. Perhaps you've seen some of the sculptured Scarabs in museums.

## Acrobats

While the buzzing wings of June-bugs and Stags loudly announce their presence, you're likely to overlook another circus performer. When you turn the slender Click Beetle on its back, it lies motionless, with folded legs. Then —quicker than you can say "metamorphosis"—it flips through the air to land on its feet. As it bounces upward, the stiff spine on its underside hits against its body with a noisy click. If you hold the beetle between two fingers you can feel the movement of the spine and hear the click as it struggles to escape.

Click Beetles, nicknamed Skip-Jacks and Snapping-

bugs, are usually middle-sized and brown or black in color. As in most families, however, there's one member who stands out. The Eyed Elater is a big pepper-and-salt colored beetle with two black eyespots on its thorax. These "eyes" are pure bluff, like the false faces children wear at Halloween, although they may serve to frighten birds away.

In the South and in tropical America there are Elaters whose eyespots light up at night. West Indians traveling through the woods sometimes tie these "fire beetles" to their ankles or toes, using them in place of flashlights. In parts of Mexico women wear them as living jewels, fastening them to their dresses or arranging them in their hair. Three or four Elaters in a bottle give enough light to read by.

Although these adult acrobats are amusing, few people like their larvae. Skinny hard-shelled creatures, they are the Wire-worms who live in the ground and feed on roots and young shoots of garden plants. Once more the Eyed Elater is an exception. Its two-inch long larva prefers rotting wood for a home and other insects as a steady diet.

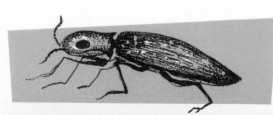

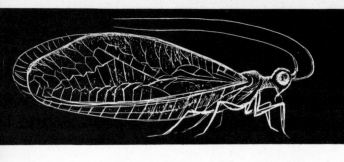

## Lions Who Have Wings

Now, ladies and gentlemen, step right up and meet the lions! Two different kinds of lions in your yard and——

"Real, honest-to-goodness ones?" You sound doubtful. "The roaring kind with whiskers and manes and tails?"

Real, honest-to-goodness INSECT lions. Quiet but fierce creatures with curving jaws and enormous appetites. Real lions that you can feed and tame and keep as pets.

From spring until late in fall watch for the frail green Lacewings whirring about your light. They have filmy wings that give off rainbow tints, long, slender antennae and bulging golden eyes. Altogether they are so delicate and lovely that children nickname them Fairy-flies.

"But what does this have to do with lions?" you interrupt.

Everything. The delicate Lacewing is the mother of a lion. Not just one lion either, but a whole hungry herd of them. All day long she hides among grass blades or under the leaves of trees. Rousing at sunset, she mates and starts laying eggs. Lion eggs.

Each egg is a work of art. The mother-to-be touches the tip of her body to the surface of a leaf and forces out a sticky drop of liquid. Raising her abdomen, she pulls up the liquid until it forms a slender silken thread. It's like the thread of syrup that you drop from a spoon when you're making candy.

REAL SIZE

At the tip of the thread she lays her oval, greenish egg. For an instant, until the thread hardens, she holds the egg in place. Then, with a jerky motion, she pulls her abdomen away. Together, egg and thread look like a balloon on a string. She completes a second and a third until she has laid several dozen in an evening and perhaps six hundred in the month that she lives as an adult.

Finding your first lion egg is not easy because they are so small. After you have spotted one, however, you'll begin to see them on leaves everywhere. You can also go into the egg business by capturing a lady Lacewing. She'll lay nice fresh eggs for you on the sides and bottom and even the lid of the jar in which you keep her.

Many books on insects explain that the Lacewing places each egg at the tip of a separate stem to prevent the larva from devouring its brothers and sisters as soon as it hatches. Some Lacewings, however, haven't read the books. These ignorant insects lay a dozen or more eggs—a whole cluster of little balloons—atop a single stem. When the larvae hatch there's a real battle to see who-eats-who first.

When the larvae hatch you'll meet the Aphidlion. At first glance it doesn't look like much. No mane, no tail, no roar. But it's probably the toughest creature for its size in the animal world. Just watch its needle-sharp jaws when it starts feeding on a colony of Aphids!

If you don't know what an Aphid is, any gardener in your neighborhood will tell you. With flashing eyes and pointing finger, she'll lead you to clusters of minute insects which suck the juices of her roses. Or her tomato

LACEWING EGGS

plants. Or her nasturtiums. True-blue gardeners feel toward Aphids the way housekeepers do toward Clothes Moths. They even call them "plant lice."

The newly hatched Aphidlion isn't much larger than its prey. But its pincer jaws quickly seize the soft-bodied insect and pierce its skin. Holding the Aphid up in the air, the lion sucks its body juices until there's nothing left inside. Then it tosses it away, as you would discard the skin of a grape. All along the stem of a plant, there's a trail of empty skins. Some species of Aphidlion cover themselves with these skins, perhaps as camouflage.

One Aphid, ten Aphids, fifty, and still the little lion hunts for food. It molts, grows bigger—and even hungrier. If you're raising one, you'll grow tired of finding Aphids long before the larva does. It eats several hundred meals before it says "Enough." When it has finally had its fill, it curls up on a leaf and spins a round silken cocoon.

Weeks later a pale pupa cuts a lid in the little silk house and pops out like a jack-in-the-box. Then the cycle starts all over again: Lacewing, egg, lion, Lacewing, egg, lion. The hungry Aphidlion on a chrysanthemum in fall is the great-grandchild of one you saw in spring.

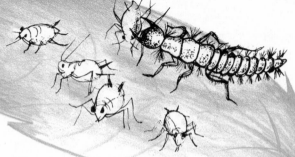

APHIDLION EATING APHIDS

REAL SIZE

The other lion in the nighttime circus takes longer to grow up. Its mother joins the parade to lights in midsummer. She's a graceful creature with transparent speckled wings, looking much like a dragonfly. She lives for only a few days, laying her tiny eggs on the surface of the ground. Her offspring are Antlions.

Before you start on an Antlion hunt it's well to be armed. Not with rifles and pith helmets, but with a spoon, a strainer, and a wide-mouthed jar. The lion you're looking for leaves a trail in sandy soil. You can track it to its lair by hunting under overhanging house eaves or rock ledges for shallow pits in the sand. Sometimes the pits are two inches across. In other places, they are only dimples, looking as if they had been made by drops of rain.

With a scoop of your spoon, dig under one of these pits. You've captured a lion. Or have you? The insect's color is so close to that of sand grains that it's hard to be sure. Here's where Weapon Number Two comes in handy. If the sand sifts through the strainer, it's sand. If it's too big for the holes, it's an Antlion—playing possum just as hard as it can play. Not until you put it in a jar, on top of a layer of sand, will it begin to move.

This lizardlike, long-jawed, short-legged creature will never get ahead in the world. It can only walk backwards. Backwards in circles, backwards in spirals, backwards into the sand. Tail first, it wriggles underground. Long after it is hidden from view, you can still see tiny fountains of sand spurting up. It is using its head for a shovel to dig a cone-shaped trap.

When the trap is completed it hides underneath it. With endless patience it waits for days, months, even years until an ant or other small insect ambles along. Ambles along and falls into the trap.

The sloping, shifting walls of sand make it difficult for the ant to escape. If it shows signs of succeeding, the lion bombards it with sand grains until it slides to the bottom of the pit. Then the curving jaws of the hunter snap closed. Dragging the ant under the sand, it dines at leisure. Minutes later it tosses out the shriveled remains of its victim. And settles back to wait for another.

One way to follow the antics of an Antlion is to put it in a bowl of sugar where its bumpy, hairy body can be clearly seen against the fine white grains. You can watch its backward bows and twisting trails for a long time. After the trap is completed you will still be able to see a pair of dark jaws at the bottom of the pit, opening and closing like sugar tongs.

Remember, however, that this is only an experiment. Mothers and fathers who don't like ants in the sugar bowl aren't going to like Antlions there either. And the insect itself will be happier if it's permanently housed in an inch or two of sand.

Antlions are easy-to-keep pets. They never escape from their cages and, unlike the hungry Aphidlions, they can live for long periods without food. In fact, they're practically indestructible. One Antlion of our acquaintance, who was being brought up in a sand-filled coffee can, spent days in a refrigerator before its absent-minded keeper discovered its whereabouts!

You can raise an Antlion until, after two or three years of larval life, it gets ready to spin a cocoon. Can you

ANTLION LARVA

REAL SIZE

ANTLION ADULTS

ANTLION LARVAE

imagine making a bed on the beach without getting sand between the sheets or under the blankets or in your hair? Sounds impossible, doesn't it? But that's no trick at all compared to what this impossible insect does. The Antlion spins its cocoon UNDERNEATH the sand, combining sand and silk until it has constructed a round ball. The outside of the ball looks like coarse sandpaper. Inside, where the pupa rests and changes to an adult, there's not one single grain of sand.

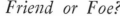

LEAFHOPPERS

REAL SIZE

REAL SIZE

*Friend or Foe?*

At the tail end of the circus parade underneath your light there's an odd assortment of performers. Some are gaudy Leafhoppers, no more than half an inch long. They come in a whole range of colors: green, red and yellow stripes, bright blue. If you try to pick one up, it will side-step, then quickly leap away. Near these insect kangaroos there is a narrow-waisted creature with trailing tails and a stinger longer than its body. It's an Ichneumon Wasp.

After you've looked closely at Leafhopper and wasp, see if you can guess which is an enemy to man and which a friend. You choose the Leafhopper for a companion?

You'd rather have nothing to do with the wasp? You couldn't be more wrong.

In the eyes of farmer and gardener, the little Leafhopper is a serious insect pest. With its pointed beak it pierces the leaves of plants and greedily sucks their juices. One Leafhopper can't do much damage, but when there are thousands sucking away, the plants often wilt and die. Even worse is the fact that Leafhoppers spread disease. They infect whole fields of potatoes, peach orchards, flower gardens, by carrying viruses from sick plants to healthy ones. Nicknamed Dodgers and Sharpshooters, they can fly for considerable distances as well as hop.

The wasp with the businesslike-looking stinger is a *parasite*. Most parasites are lazy characters who, while doing no work themselves, live off the efforts of others. The lady Ichneumon who is pictured on this page is clever rather than lazy. She uses her stinger to drill inches deep into the trunk of a tree. Not just any old tree, but one which is infested with wood-borers. Her eggs are laid in the wood-borers' burrow and her larvae feed on the young borers. Since the borers damage the trees and the Ichneumons damage the borers, everyone is grateful for their parasitic habits. Except the borers.

Incidentally, there's no need to worry about the Ichneumon stinger. More correctly called an ovipositor, or egg layer, it is NEVER used to attack human beings.

ICHNEUMON WASP

## Chapter Five

## A NIGHT'S FISHING

Where else do insects go when they are answering the siren call of light? That depends on where they came from in the first place. That depends on whether they were born in field or park or garden—or whether they hatched from eggs laid in the water. If you try fishing with a light near a pond, you can catch all kinds of new winged creatures.

In spring or early summer you may see thousands of Mayflies rising from the water, thousands weaving through the air in a graceful mating flight—and thousands of dead insects a day or two later.

Delicate, slender-bodied, with shiny, gauzy wings and threadlike tails, their legs are weak, their mouth parts useless. They cannot eat during their adult life and they have no weapons to defend themselves.

They are the easiest of all winged insects to catch—and Mayfly collectors live everywhere. Toads and spiders, birds and fish snap them up. In some places fishermen even import English Mayflies for United States trout to feed on. After the trout eat the insects, the fishermen bait their hooks with artificial Mayflies. Then it's the fishermen's turn to eat the trout.

Mayflies also provide food for thought. Their scientific name, *Ephemeridae,* goes back to ancient Greece. In Greek mythology, the Ephemerides were creatures who lived for one day. Observing the sudden "birth" and death of a Mayfly swarm, the Greeks were sure that the life span of these frail creatures was only twenty-four hours. For centuries since then philosophers and poets have praised their short and merry lives.

MAYFLY

It's too bad to spoil a poetic fancy, but Mayflies are long-lived compared to many insects. They often take two or three years to develop and some species spend the better part of their lives burrowing in mud!

After mating, the female Mayfly returns to the water to lay eggs. The minute eggs hatch into nymphs, soft-bodied larvae with feathery gills and tails. Feeding on microscopic plants, they grow and shed their skins. When their wings are fully formed, they swim to the surface of the water. One more molt and their gills disappear. Although they are winged creatures making a wobbly flight to land, they are not yet full-fledged adults. They must shed their skins for a final time before they can mate. At last, after long years in the water, they are ready for their short but merry lives.

MAYFLY NYMPH

MIDGE

## Dancing Flies

Poets never write about the swarms of Midges who dance at twilight. Nor do philosophers feel philosophic or scientists scientific when these tiny flies gather at their lights. Almost everyone wishes them a short life or, better still, none at all.

Midges have a bad name, in fact a whole series of bad names ranging from Punkies and No-see-ums to some which are unprintable. If you've ever spent a night by the shore of a pond when Midges were swarming, you'll understand why. They are so small that they can fly through ordinary window screens. When a million of them invade your bedroom, the only thing to do is to put out the light, pull the covers over your head, and go to sleep.

Actually, that's not fair. Most species of Midges don't bite at all and those who do aren't nearly as bad as their big cousins, the mosquitoes. It's just that there are SO many of them. Sometimes they fly in such huge crowds that the buzzing of their tiny wings sounds like a water-fall.

Midge mothers also lay eggs in water. Their caterpillar-like larvae build silk-and-mud tubes in which to live. Perhaps you've seen these tiny tubes fastened to dead leaves or stones at the bottom of a pond. The best-known tube makers are bright red, colored by hemoglobin which isn't very different from the coloring matter in your own blood. Most people call them Blood-worms. Don't confuse them, however, with another Blood-worm, a real worm who builds tubes in the mucky waters of a pond. You can tell the Midges from the worms—although you may have to use a magnifying glass to do so—because the insect larvae have distinct heads and legs but the worms are, well, wormlike.

While the magnifying glass is nearby, take a look at a grown-up Midge. With its rainbow-tinted wings and its feathery antennae, it's surprisingly pretty, isn't it? It's also the first two-winged night insect you've seen. This means that it's a true fly, related to the House Fly and the Horse Fly and the Crane Fly, but not to the Mayfly or the Firefly or the butterfly, all of whom have four wings.

The Crane Fly is another insect of ponds and marshy woods who will come to your light. The first time you see a swarm of them bobbing over the water at twilight you'll be tempted to run and hide. They look like every-body's bad dream of a giant mosquito. Actually, they are slow-moving awkward creatures without stingers who wouldn't even hurt a fly.

As adults they rarely eat, although sometimes they sip nectar from flowers. Their gangling legs trail behind them when they float through the air and break off easily if you pick them up. Crane Fly larvae are legless, wormlike crea-tures who live in damp soil or in the water.

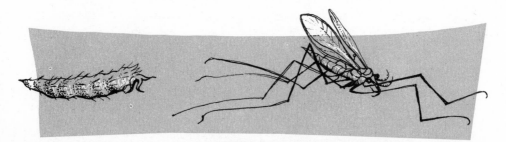

## Trailer Builders

The Caddisfly is another pond dweller. NOT a fly, it is a four-winged creature who closely resembles a moth. Only when you notice one at rest with its long antennae pointing forward and its wings folded over its body like a tent do you realize that it belongs to a different order.

The tan or gray hairy-winged adults are not particularly interesting. It's their young you will want to meet. Caddisfly babies are really caterpillars who spend their larval lives under water, in homes which they build for themselves. Each species has its own building style. Some build with pebbles or sand grains or tiny shells, cementing the materials together to make neat mosaic walls. One well-to-do insect who lived in a creek in Montana built a home for itself with tiny nuggets of gold!

Other Caddisflies prefer vegetable matter, building log cabins of crisscrossed twigs or decorating tubes with bits of leaves cut to proper size. In fast-moving streams, some species spin cup-shaped nets which are used to catch food. All of these homes are cemented together with silk which pours from their mouths in a sticky sheet and hardens quickly under water.

A Caddisfly has a big advantage over most homeowners. Wherever it goes, its house goes, too. With head and forelegs protruding, it lumbers across the bottom of a pond or clambers up a plant stem. Eating as it travels, it feeds on decayed leaves and sometimes on other insects.

CADDISFLY LARVA

If danger threatens, it retreats indoors, with its hooked rear legs holding on tightly to its home.

As it grows, it enlarges its house, adding section after section to the front end. When it is ready to pupate, it spins doors of silk netting, doors which let water in but keep unwelcome visitors out. The insect's final transformation takes place above water. Floating to the surface, the pupa crawls onto a twig. Its skin splits and its new wings expand and dry.

Entomologists have performed all sorts of experiments with these undersized architects. They have evicted log-cabin builders from their houses and given them only sand and pebbles to build with. Or they have offered twigs and leaves to mason Caddisflies. Making the best of a bad situation, the insects build strange-looking structures. In desperation sometimes, they even build with the leaves supplied to them for food. When this happens, their aquarium mates—like Hansel and Gretel with the gingerbread house—nibble at their green roofs and walls.

## Fisherman's Friend

One of the most striking water insects who comes to lights in midsummer is the Dobsonfly. It's big—often five inches long—and it has a curious "neck," like a high collar, which permits it to turn its head every which way, at impossible angles. When a lady Dobson pauses at a light, she spreads out her gray spotted wings behind her in queenly fashion, as if she were displaying peacock feathers.

CADDISFLY

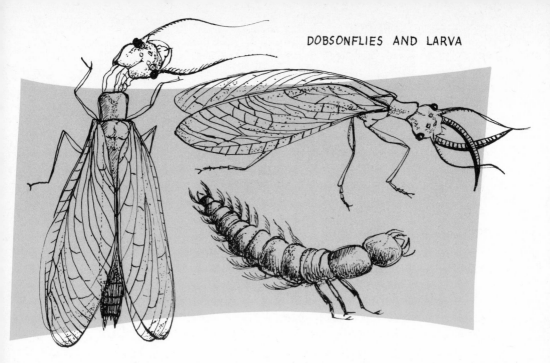

The male has curving ice-tong jaws. Although they look frightening, they're quite harmless. As a matter of fact, he uses them only to hug the female during mating. Her stubby jaws are much more likely to pinch, if you handle her carelessly.

Dobsonflies live only a few nights as winged adults. After mating, each female lays thousands of chalky white eggs on rocks or tree branches near a stream, sometimes so many of them that the stones seem to be splashed with whitewash. She'll also lay eggs in a jar, if you imprison her at the right time.

When the larvae hatch, they tumble into the water. Their parents never eat, but the babies start right in to make up for the fast. Hiding under stones in swift-running streams, they catch and devour all the water insects they can lay jaws on. They eat, and they are eaten. Fishermen, who call them Hellgrammites, use them as live bait for bass and other fresh-water game fish.

BACKSWIMMER

In May or June, as its third birthday draws near, the Hellgrammite crawls to shore. Strong-legged and strong-jawed, with a rough brown body, it looks for a place to pupate. Avoiding the light, it travels by night and hides during the day. After a restless search, it settles down to build an earthen cell underneath a stone or log. Several weeks later it is transformed into an adult insect.

## A Bug Is a Bug

Late in summer, when ponds dry up or become over-crowded, some of their insect inhabitants fly off to hunt new homes. Flying at night, they are often sidetracked by the siren call of an electric light. This is when you'll meet the water bugs and beetles.

Water bugs are really bugs, flat-bodied insects with sharp, jointed beaks and two pairs of wings. The smallest of these night fliers are the Water Boatmen and Back-swimmers. When you see them on land, with their legs and wings folded, they remind you of their relatives, the Leaf-hoppers. In water, however, they're fast swimmers. The Backswimmer does a smooth, steady backstroke while the Water Boatman swims on its belly, using its oarlike hind legs as if they were flippers.

Lacking gills, both insects carry a silvery bubble of air along with them when they travel under water—their own version of the Aqua-lung. Most Water Boatmen are vege-tarians, but the Backswimmers eat tadpoles, salamanders,

WATER BOATMEN

and their insect neighbors. Even though they are small, their curved beaks are sharp enough to pierce your skin.

Backswimmer and Water Boatman eggs are laid on water plants, but the eggs of some species of Giant Water Bug have a more unusual location. The mother bug lays her eggs on the father's back, fastening them securely with a special waterproof glue. No matter how hard the unwilling baby sitter tries, he can't shake them off. He must swim around with his nursery until the eggs hatch into little bugs. Little bugs which quickly grow into big ones.

As bugs go, Giant Water Bugs are BIG. In tropical America some of them are five inches long. The United States ones are less than half that size, but they're big enough! Pale brown, with grasping forelegs which look like crab claws, they catch all kinds of water creatures—dragonfly nymphs, snails, and good-sized fish. Plunging their beaks into their victims, they inject a poisonous saliva which paralyzes and then kills. They can be serious pests in fish hatcheries.

The Giant Water Bug is an air breather. It stores a supply of air under its wings, poking its abdomen above water when it needs to refuel. Although most of its life is spent in ponds or streams, it's a strong flier. When it's on the wing, it may follow the call of a light for many miles. Sometimes Giant Water Bugs are found in large numbers in cities, underneath street lights or on top of tall buildings. That's why these flying submarines are often called Electric Light Bugs. They have also been nicknamed Fish-Killers and Toe-Biters!

GIANT WATER BUGS

WATER
SCAVENGER
BEETLE

DIVING
BEETLE

## Cannibals

The Predacious Diving Beetle and the Water Scavenger Beetle are almost as big and almost as tough as Giant Water Bugs. According to the dictionary, predacious means "living by plundering." That's a good description of the life of these beetles. They hunt all of their small and middle-sized neighbors—tadpoles, salamanders, mussels, fish, and other beetles. Because they are cannibals from the day they are born, scientists studying their habits have to raise each bloodthirsty little larva in a separate aquarium.

Unlike the water bugs the beetles have no beaks. More streamlined than June-bugs or Stags, their polished bodies are so slippery that they're hard to hold onto and so shiny that they reflect images of water plants and stones as if they were mirrors. Although they appear to be black when you see them under water, many are brown or olive green.

When at rest, the Predacious Diving Beetle hangs head downward, with the tip of its elytra poking out of water. Before it dives, it raises its wings to collect a supply of air underneath them. The Water Scavenger has an opposite system. It rests with its head above water, using its antennae to trap a bubble of air when it's ready for a swim. The shiny air bubble which covers the lower surface of the beetle's body looks like a piece of cellophane.

All of the water beetles have a complete metamorphosis. Diving Beetle eggs are laid singly in the leaves of water plants while the mother Water Scavenger spins a waterproof cocoon for her offspring. Sometimes she carries the cocoon around with her. More often, she attaches it to the underside of a lily pad or sets it afloat on the surface of the pond. It is peaceful aboard the little silk boat until the eggs hatch and the babies begin to eat each other!

The larvae of the Predacious Diving Beetle, called Water-tigers, are skinny, big-jawed wrigglers. They can lick any creature their size who lives in the water—and many who are bigger. Their sturdy legs and snakelike bodies permit them to crawl and leap as well as swim. When they are full-grown, they travel to shore to pupate in damp ground at the water's edge. The adult beetles return to the water to feed and mate, flying abroad only at night.

Ferocious as these insects are, they have no way to protect themselves against ducks and turtles and men. In ponds in Asia, they are raised and harvested for food. To Chinese children, a dried Diving Beetle tastes as good as a chocolate bar.

DIVING BEETLE

WATER SCAVENGER BEETLE

DIVING BEETLE LARVA

## In a Fish Bowl

Except for the Dobsonflies, whose young insist on fast-moving streams, all of these night-flying sailors can be kept as pets. With a net or a kitchen strainer, you can trap them in shallow water at almost any time of the year and raise them in fish bowls, aquariums, or even glass baking dishes. They're far easier to raise than tropical fish and considerably less expensive.

The meat eaters can be fed on mosquito larvae, tadpoles, and snails, and even on bits of hamburger. (One scientist kept a Diving Beetle alive for three years with scraps of raw meat.) The vegetarians will be satisfied with water plants and with the microscopic goodies that abound in pond water.

Since most of the insects come to the surface for air, you don't have to worry about elaborate aerating equipment either. The only thing you DO have to worry about is separating the vegetarians from the meat eaters and keeping your own fingers clear of the sharp beaks of the bugs.

You can even try experiments with the Caddisfly

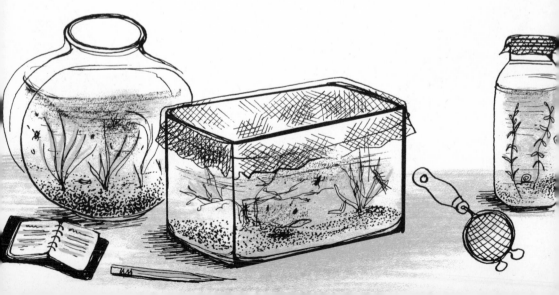

builders the way the scientists do. Will all the masons build with rice grains, or the carpenters with pine needles? Another experiment is to take away the home of one of the Caddis larvae in the fish bowl. When there are more larvae than houses, it's like a game of Musical Chairs.

If you give houseroom to a pail of water insects, you will soon notice strange noises and smells. Many of the bugs and beetles make squeaky sounds when they're in the water. They rub their legs together or their abdomens against their wings. And when you hold one slippery beetle in your hand it gives off a milky fluid which smells like apple cider. Perhaps the noises are the mating calls of males. Probably the beetle hopes you'll drop it if it sprays you with its perfume.

Perhaps. Probably. There's a great deal still to be learned about these creatures. The biggest question of all is—how do they find their way to water? How are they able to travel from one pond to another in the dark of night? From a dried-up stream to the water-logged cellar of an unfinished house? From the woods where they have mated to the shore where they will lay their eggs?

Some scientists say that they are *hydrotropic*, that they MUST travel toward water, the way plant roots do. When they've said that, they haven't explained very much. Other scientists guess that they have more senses (not more sense!) than people have. That in addition to sight and smell and taste and touch and hearing, they have a special water-finding sense. But if you ask where this sense is located and how it works, they can only shrug their shoulders. Perhaps this is something that you or one of your friends will find out about some day.

# Chapter Six

## HUNTING AND TRAPPING

When your mother makes out her shopping list this week, ask her if she'll buy a few things for you. "Nothing very much," you can casually explain. "Just some rotten peaches, a pound or so of overripe bananas, a jar of molasses, and a box of brown sugar."

"Oh yes," you must politely add, "some decaying meat would be nice. And I really must have a dead mouse or bird, but perhaps I'd better find those myself instead of bothering the people at the store."

"Perhaps you had better," your mother will doubtless agree in a grim voice. "Perhaps you had better explain yourself RIGHT NOW."

Nothing could be simpler. It's time to turn off the light, flip the switch, extinguish the illumination. It's time to find new ways to hunt the creatures of the night. To try the siren song of nectar and the lure of rotting meat.

## Homemade Nectar

Nectar is the sweet stuff in flowers that bees like to sip. It's also the favorite food of many night insects. Since even the supermarket doesn't sell it, you'll have to make your own. There are many different recipes.

"Mash six rotten peaches and four overripe bananas. Stir well, adding a tablespoon of molasses and two of brown sugar."

Or "Strain four overripe peaches and six rotten bananas. Add two tablespoons of molasses and one of brown sugar."

It really doesn't matter which recipe you follow so long as the nectar tastes sweet and smells strong, the sweeter and stronger the better. After it has fermented for a few hours, it should be a gloppy mixture, like fudge that hasn't hardened or ice cream that's beginning to melt. It won't look like the nectar that the Greek gods used to drink, but it will be just right for six-legged diners.

Late in the afternoon it will be time to set the banquet table, a process that insect collectors call *sugaring*. With a whitewash brush, paint patches of nectar on fence posts and the trunks of trees, selecting trees perhaps ten feet apart and mapping out a briar-free, boulder-free path which you'll be able to follow at night. Before doing this, it's wise to inform your neighbors of your plan so that you won't be mistaken for a prowler. One well-known entomologist barely escaped with his life when he sugared some trees behind a farmer's chicken coop!

## Like Christmas Morning

At last supper is over and the sun has dropped below the horizon. A cloud shadows the curving new moon and the humid air promises a thunderstorm. Dark, hot, humid, it's a perfect night for hunting insects.

Armed with a flashlight, you trudge along the path. Your companion nudges you with his elbow. "It's like Christmas morning," he whispers. "You know, when you're coming downstairs and wondering what you'll find on the tree."

"Ssh," you whisper back, feeling the same way. Your heartbeat quickens as you approach the first sugared tree. Will there be any diners?

Cautiously you raise your flashlight to a dark spot on the tree bark. There ARE diners, three of them, four of them. Scarcely daring to breathe, you watch others wing in. Silent, ghostlike creatures, they settle down to sample the feast. An army of ants crawls up from the ground, chasing away a beetle who has dared to join them. Other insects, flat-bodied, long-legged, scurry from your light.

Most of the diners are Owlets, middle-sized, hairy-bodied moths with slender antennae and golden eyes. These eyes, glowing like tiny headlights, seem to light up the dark trunk of the tree, as if they were battery-powered.

Actually, it's the battery in your flashlight that provides the light. The Owlets' eyes have a special mirrorlike layer of cells that reflect the flashlight beam. When the flashlight is turned off, the eye shine vanishes. Cats' eyes gleam in the same way at night. So do frogs' and owls'.

UNDERWING MOTHS

The Owlets make up the largest family of American moths. The ones you'll meet most often—at lighted windows as well as on sugared trees—are plain-looking creatures with tan or gray wings. Their young are Cutworms, smooth-skinned fat caterpillars who usually curl up head to tail in the soil during the day and come out at night to feed. Your gardening friends can tell you all about the Cutworms who chew through the stems of their tender young tomatoes or beans, cutting off the plants at the surface of the ground just as they're starting to grow.

The beauty queens of the Owlet family are the Underwings. When you see them at first with their wings folded over their abdomens, they don't look like anything special. But wait! After they have drunk deeply, when they're a bit intoxicated by the heady nectar that you are serving, they'll spread out their wings. Their forewings match the tree bark, but their bright underwings are banded with yellow or raspberry red. People can't see these colors when the moths are flying in the dark, but perhaps other Underwings can.

## Super-Bug

One of the insects who scrambled away when you first flashed a light on the sugared tree is still hiding nearby, its long antennae poking out from a crack in the bark. You'll have to move quickly to catch it because its flat waxed body is as slippery as a watermelon seed.

Black or brown, it has two pairs of folded wings and a head that's half hidden by the front of its thorax. Its critics say that it has a hangdog look, that it hides its head because it's ashamed to look at you. Its admirers speak of it as Super-bug.

"But what IS it?" you want to know. "It doesn't look quite like a beetle or a bug or——"

Alas, it's that most despised of all insects, the cockroach. Its scientific name, *Blatta*, means "insect that shuns the light." Because it likes damp, dark, warm places, it often hides in people's homes, in cracks in the floors, in cellars and under kitchen sinks, coming out at night to feed.

If you live in the city, where colonies of cockroaches move from one apartment to the other, you're bound to be prejudiced against them. Not only do they eat your food and garbage but they leave behind an unpleasant musty smell.

COCKROACHES

Not every cockroach is a house roach, however. Most of them live outdoors close to their cousins, the crickets and grasshoppers. They hide under stones or loose bark during the daytime hours. When they're not feeding on garbage, there's nothing dirty or disgusting about them. As a matter of fact they spend a good part of their time cleaning themselves just as cats do. They lick their antennae and feet and then use their spiny legs to comb the rest of their bodies.

Female cockroaches lay their eggs in egg cases, neat brown packages which they carry around with them until the eggs are almost ready to hatch. The young are small copies of their parents. Their long legs carry them swiftly over the ground. Their flat bodies permit them to hide in the tiniest imaginable crack and their sensitive antennae warn of the presence of danger—and of food.

Indoors or out, cockroaches eat ANYTHING—from dried fish in a Laplander hut in the Arctic to filet mignon in an expensive hotel at the Equator. Fish and filet, eggshells and orange rinds, butter and grease—to say nothing of paint, paste, starched linen curtains, and the gold lettering on the backs of books. Because they are so hardy and so easy to feed, scientists often raise them as laboratory animals, using them in experiments instead of white mice.

The most despised of all insects, the cockroach is also the most successful. Three hundred million years ago roaches scuttled up the skinny trunks of fern trees and flew across swamps which would some day be beds of coal. There were cockroaches in caves when men first moved indoors and clothed themselves in animal skins. There were cockroaches in Egyptian tombs and in the columned temples of Greece. In the first century A.D., Pliny, a Roman naturalist, reported on the roach. "It is mostly found in baths," he wrote, adding quite incorrectly that it is "produced from the humid vapors which arise therefrom."

Cockroaches traveled from Asia to Europe and from Africa to America. They sailed before the mast with Columbus, stowed away on the Mayflower, and settled New Amsterdam with the Dutch. The great-great-—a hundred times great—grandma of the roaches feeding on your sugar mixture probably crossed the Atlantic from West Africa in the hold of a slave ship.

Insects with a glorious past, cockroaches have a future as well. Quite recently roaches from East Africa were found in considerable numbers in New York City. These roaches wouldn't be caught dead in any old sink or garbage pail. Instead, they had set up housekeeping inside of TV sets. With electronic tubes keeping them warm, they dine in comfort on glue and insulated wires. Doubtless these TV roaches or other members of their enterprising family will be the first passengers on a rocket to Mars!

## We Prefer Meat

Many night insects aren't attracted by either lights or sugaring. If the Carrion Beetles were able to rhyme, they would doubtless explain:

*Sugar tastes sweet*
*But we prefer meat*

            or       *Nectar is nice.*
                      *So are dead mice.*

These beetles survey the countryside at night, hunting for dead animals. To meet some of them you have only to sink a narrow-necked jar into the ground, its top level with the surface, and bait the jar with a scrap of decaying meat. When you look in the jar the next morning, you'll find beetles galore. In spite of their unpleasant food tastes, they are handsome creatures, their shiny black bodies marked with bright yellow or red.

Sexton Beetles, the most remarkable members of the Carrion Beetle family, aren't satisfied with decaying meat in a jar. They are insect gravediggers who bury the carcasses that they find in order to store food for their children. They will tackle any small dead creature—a mouse, a bird, a shrew, a garter snake.

With antennae thrust out, a Sexton Beetle flies through the woods until it has located its prey. Spiraling to the ground, it folds its wings and sets to work. First, there's a quick survey of the situation. The beetle inspects the mouse, touching its fur with forefeet and feelers. Then, rolling over on its back with legs extended, it squeezes under the carcass. It lifts up the mouse with its feet, shifting the dead body a fraction of an inch as it slides along underneath it.

Apparently satisfied with the size and condition of the carcass, the beetle emerges from its far side. Righting itself, it begins to explore the surrounding earth. Is the soil rocky? Are there too many roots? Using its forelegs as shovels, it digs in several different spots. With head and body, it plows the earth until it finds clear soil.

Scurrying back to the mouse, it squeezes under the car-

CARRION BEETLES

cass again, as if it were taking measurements. Another trip to the plowed area for a few minutes of digging, and then it returns to the mouse once more. By this time it has been joined by another black and red beetle. Lying on their backs, with their twelve strong legs pushing against the mouse's fur, they painstakingly shift the carcass. A quarter of an inch, a half an inch, an inch—the mouse's body slowly wobbles toward the plowed earth.

Hours pass as the two beetles push and pull and pedal the dead weight above them until they have moved it to its burial site. Still working from underneath the mouse, they shift the soil particles so that the carcass sinks below the ground. Even after the mouse has disappeared from view, the beetles continue to dig. The grave is not completed until the carcass is two inches underneath the earth.

In a tunnel adjoining the burial chamber, the female Sexton now lays her eggs. Both parents remain underground, preserving the mouse so that it doesn't decay and guarding it against earthworms and other insects. When the eggs hatch, the adults feed the larvae and even prepare the rooms in which they later pupate.

SEXTON BEETLES

REAL SIZE

FEMALE MOSQUITO

*Bzzz!*

Are you ready for another hunting expedition? This evening you won't need nectar or dead meat. This evening YOU are the bait. Your arms and legs, your perspiring forehead, the soft skin at the back of your neck—every square bare inch of you is shouting "Supper's ready! Come and get it!" to the most persistent and provoking, the most irritating and tormenting of all night insects—the mosquito.

There's one buzzing about your head right now, looking for a good spot on which to settle. "Fee fi fo fum" she happily hums as she lands on your arm. Then—silence. Folding her single pair of wings over her abdomen, she thrusts her daggerlike beak into your skin. After injecting some of her own saliva to keep your blood from clotting, she begins to suck. If you don't interrupt her, she'll sip your blood for more than a minute, until her swelling abdomen looks like a round red ball. And if you do interrupt her, she'll soon return to sample your other arm.

Will it make your itchy red welt feel better if you know that you have been bitten by a mother-to-be? Most of the time she feeds on plant juices and nectar, but she cannot produce eggs unless, at least once in her short life, she sips warm animal blood. A cat's or dog's would satisfy her needs, but your hairless thin skin is a more tempting target.

After spending a few evenings digesting her meal, she looks for a suitable place to lay eggs. There are two thousand different kinds of mosquitoes in the world, but the House Mosquito whom you're most likely to encounter lays her eggs on the surface of stagnant water, gluing them together so that they form a raft.

You can find these rafts in all sorts of places around your home—in a neighbor's wading pool, in your small sister's watering can, in a rowboat in which rain water has collected. At first they look like tiny black specks floating on the water. When you look at them with a magnifying glass you'll see the rows of eggs standing on end. Less than twenty-four hours after they are laid, the top of each egg flips up and the babies pop out.

The larvae can be raised in an ordinary drinking glass, with a piece of gauze over the top to prevent the adults from escaping later on. A pinch of mud from the bottom of a pond or a minute amount of bread crumbs will supply them with food. And if you find that you have too many larvae you can always put some in an aquarium with fish or water bugs.

The big-headed bristly mosquito babies swim through the water by wriggling their slender bodies. Instead of gills they have long breathing tubes at the tips of their abdomens. Most of the time they hang head-down, with these snorkel-like tubes poking above the surface of the water. The shadow of your hand will send them wriggling to the bottom of the glass and if they stay under water long enough they will drown.

MALE MOSQUITO

85

REAL SIZE

In midsummer the wrigglers are full-grown within a week. (It takes longer during the cool weather in spring and fall.) Perhaps you'll be able to see the larval skin split and a pupa emerge. Of all insect 'tween-agers, this hump-backed gnome is the funniest-looking. Lighter than water, it floats at the surface, breathing through two short tubes just behind its head. If danger threatens, it wriggles toward the bottom, then quickly floats upward again. After two days of pupal life the humped back splits and an adult works its way out.

One advantage of a raise-your-own-mosquito project is that it gives you a chance to see a male. He's a gentle creature who never bites, who doesn't even have a mouth sharp enough to pierce your skin. His evenings are spent sipping nectar and listening with his feathery antennae for a female's mating song.

When he hears her high-pitched hum, the plumes on his antennae begin to vibrate. Turning his head in the direction of the sound, he flies to find his lady. His antennae work in much the same way as those of the male Silk Moths, except that the mosquito follows sound instead of smell.

The female mosquito doesn't really sing. The insistent whine that attracts her mate and keeps you awake on hot summer nights is made by the rapid vibration of her wings. Each species of mosquito produces a different sound, usually in the neighborhood of high C on the piano.

In recent years scientists have made recordings of these sounds. By playing the recordings, they can lure mosquitoes to traps which electrocute them. The inventor of one mosquito trap thinks that it can be used indoors as well as out if radio stations would broadcast mosquito songs instead of dance music.

MOSQUITO EGGS

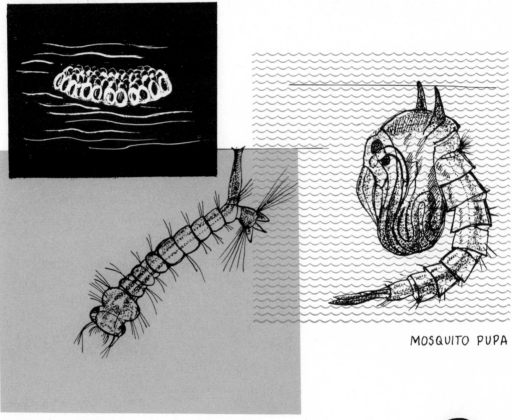

MOSQUITO PUPA

MOSQUITO LARVA

REAL SIZE

## Chapter Seven

### A WALK TO NOWHERE

Did you ever take a walk to nowhere? Not to school or to visit a friend, but a walk up the hill, across the road, through the woods—a walk to no-place-special to see what you can see? Even if you've done this during the day, try it some evening after supper. Anything is likely to happen!

There are lights flashing on and off everywhere. Green lights twinkling under the trees, yellow ones glowing in the tall grass. It's dusk and the fireflies are sending out signals. They're talking to each other.

"Where are you?" The male's taillight flashes the question.

"Right here." The female's winking light replies.

You don't believe it? Well, sit down on the grass and join in a conversation. The light blinking a few yards over your head comes from a male firefly who's looking for a mate. Instead of following her scent or her sound as moths and mosquitoes do, he's using his eyes and his light to find her.

Wait for two seconds after he blinks and then answer him with a short signal from your flashlight. Has he seen you? Yes, for his taillight is flashing again. One-and-two-and-it's-time-for-your-reply. Another flash and he's dropping down, headed in your direction. One-and-two-and-blink-your-light-once-more. He's flying lower and lower. A flash from his tail, an answer from you—and he lands on your hand!

A brown, soft-bodied beetle, only half an inch long, his scientific name is *Photinus pyralis*. On almost any midsummer night he will respond to a light in the grass that flashes two seconds after his own.

You won't be able to fool all of the fireflies all of the time, however. Each kind has its own special code. Some give several short flashes in rapid succession while others wait as long as ten seconds before replying. The wingless females of one species climb to the top of a blade of grass and shine their beacons steadily until they have attracted a mate. These grublike creatures who look more like larvae than full-grown beetles are usually called Glowworms.

Firefly babies are also spoken of as Glowworms. Even before they hatch from eggs laid in the soil, they give off a faint light. Short-legged, hard-shelled, they hide under the ground during the day and come out at night to hunt. At first they eat tiny soil creatures. As they grow larger, they tackle all sorts of game—earthworms, caterpillars, and even snails.

FIREFLIES

REAL SIZE

Climbing on top of a snail shell, a Glowworm waits for long minutes until the snail pokes out its foot. As soon as this happens, the insect goes into action, using its jaws to inject poison into its prey. The paralyzed snail is unable to pull back into its shell, and the Glowworm can dine at leisure.

Glowworms usually spend two years as larvae, hibernating during the winter months. In the spring of their third year, they pupate under stones or in round huts which they build for themselves out of mud. As they change from pupae to adult beetles, the faint Glowworm glow disappears and a new bright light takes its place.

The flashing green GO light depends on two substances in the insect's abdomen, *luciferin* and *luciferase*. By combining these with oxygen from the air and other chemicals in its body, the firefly is able to turn its light on and off at will. The light itself is surprisingly efficient, wasting very little of its energy in heat the way an electric light bulb does.

In recent years scientists have collected fireflies and studied them in order to find out exactly how this cold light is made. That is, children have done the collecting —for twenty-five cents for a hundred fireflies—while the scientists dried the insects' tails, ground them to powder, and treated them with chemicals in order to separate the light-producing substances. Right now, it takes a quarter of a million fireflies to produce one ounce of pure luciferin. Some day, however, it may be possible to make the stuff artificially in a laboratory. When this happens, we'll probably start lighting our living rooms with cold firefly light.

The Japanese catch fireflies not for scientific purposes but because they enjoy watching their twinkling lights. Before a host gives an outdoor party he buys gauze-covered boxes filled with the insects, setting them free in his garden when his guests arrive. Thousands of fireflies are collected and released during the Battle of the Fireflies, an annual festival in Tokyo.

In the West as well as the East, everyone likes these tiny torchbearers. You'll find them described in serious poems about love as well as in funny rhymes. Perhaps you know the jingle about the lightning-bug:

> "The lightning-bug is a wondrous sight,
> But you'd think it has no mind;
> It pumps around in the darkest night,
> With its headlight on behind."

FIREFLIES AND THEIR LARVAE

## Follow Your Nose

As it grows darker, stand still for a moment and take a deep breath. Can you smell the strong sweet perfume of night-blooming flowers? The Nicotiana in the garden, the honeysuckle along the road, the evening primrose in the field are sending out messages, begging for visitors.

There's nectar in the deep tube of the Nicotiana and a stout-bodied, narrow-winged moth floats down to sample it. Uncurling its watch-spring tongue, the moth begins to sip. A handsome insect, gray, black, white, with spots of yellow on its abdomen, it carries pollen from one blossom to another as it feeds. Without a visit from one of these long-tongued Sphinx Moths, the Nicotiana would not be able to ripen its seed.

Often called a Hawk-moth, the Sphinx is the fastest flier of all night insects—as you may discover if you try to catch one with a net. Sometimes it feeds from mid-air, holding itself in position over a flower by the rapid motion of its wings.

The lovely, velvet-winged Sphinx who sips nectar from fragrant flowers is the parent of hungry Hornworms. Fat green caterpillars with white stripes along their sides and pointed horns growing from the tips of their tails, Hornworms feed on the leaves of tomato and tobacco plants.

Three or four inches long when it is full-grown, the caterpillar burrows into the soil to pupate. Perhaps you've seen its shiny brown pupal case which has a loop at one end like the handle of a cup. Inside this handle, the coiled tongue of the moth-to-be is formed.

SPHINX MOTH

SPHINX MOTH CATERPILLAR

OWLET MOTHS

Several of the night-blooming flowers and night-flying moths have a you-help-me-and-I'll-help-you relationship. If you flash your light on the yellow blossoms of the evening primrose, you'll probably see a small pink and yellow moth. A member of the Owlet family with the scientific name of *Rhodophora florida,* this moth fertilizes the primrose flowers as it sips their nectar. At dawn, when the flower petals close, the moth crawls inside a blossom, hiding away until evening. The yellow petals of the flower, which are tinged with pink as they fade, offer perfect concealment for the insect's bright wings.

Even more remarkable is the relationship between the Yucca plant and a tiny white moth. The straight-stalked, stiff-leaved Yucca, originally an American desert plant, is now grown in gardens all over the world. If there's one in your neighborhood, it's well worth watching at night.

Unlike the Sphinx or the Owlet who accidentally carry pollen when it sticks to their hairy bodies or wings, the female Yucca Moth deliberately collects pollen grains. With the help of special curved hooks in her mouth, she rolls them into a ball often three times as large as her head. Then she crams the ball into an open flower on the plant.

Her action isn't as unselfish as it seems because she also lays her eggs inside the flower. When her caterpillars hatch, they eat the Yucca seed that their mother helped to make. Yucca plants flourish in European gardens, but they never produce seed—because there are no Yucca Moths to do the fertilizing job!

94

YUCCA PLANT

## Birth of a Bug

Something is happening on the old fence post at the edge of the woods. There's an enormous insect clinging to a knothole near the top of the post. Its thin brown skin has split and a wet white body struggles into view. First a head with bulging green eyes and curving beak. Then slowly, ever so slowly, a broad body with glistening green and white wings appears.

Pushing forward and upward, the insect frees itself at last from its lifeless skin. Its soft body throbs as blood pumps through it. Its crumpled wings hang down, begin to straighten, their color changing to a darker green.

Nothing you do—no sound you make, no light you shine—will disturb this insect now. It's a Cicada. For perhaps four years it has been living in a burrow under the ground, feeding on tree roots, growing, molting, growing. Tonight is the night of its final transformation. It rests on the fence post, clutching its old skin as if it were riding pickaback. When the sun rises, when its body is hard and its wings dry, it will fly.

If you go back to the post in the morning you'll find the empty skin still clinging to the knothole. A stiff tan shell, it gives you a perfect picture of the insect-that-used-to-be. Sometimes you may see clusters of these ghost bugs on the branches or trunk of a tree. They are the discarded skins of Periodical Cicadas who spend seventeen years under the ground (or thirteen if they live in the South).

PERIODICAL CICADA

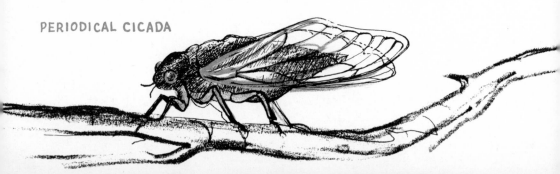

CICADA EMERGING

Unlike the common Cicada these insect Rip Van Winkles—who have red eyes and red-veined wings instead of green—crawl out of the ground in droves. Hundreds of them appear in the same area over a period of a week or two. After they mate and lay eggs, the adults die. The newly hatched young tunnel into the soil and don't show up again until seventeen years have gone by.

There are dozens of different species of Cicada all over the world, but the Periodical Cicada is found only in the United States. When the Pilgrims in Plymouth Colony saw and heard these creatures for the first time, they were horrified. They were sure that they were being visited by a swarm of locusts who would eat all their corn and grain. Because of their mistake, many people still refer to Cicadas as locusts, although a locust—really a grasshopper—is a member of an entirely different insect order.

Cicadas are harmless both to people and to crops. As a matter of fact, they're so heavy-bodied and slow-moving that all sorts of winged creatures—birds, dragonflies, wasps —feast on them. The only damage a Cicada is ever likely to do is to your nervous system. It is they who are responsible for the shrill steady buzz that you hear all day and into the evening hours during July and August. To be more accurate, it is the male Cicadas, equipped with drumlike music boxes under the bases of their wings, who make the noise. Probably it is intended as a mating call, although it continues long after mating has taken place and the lady Cicadas are busy laying eggs.

### Follow Your Flashlight

As it grows darker, you swing your flashlight from side to side, directing its beam up into the trees and down along the path. There's a flying squirrel on the branch of an oak. Spreading its furry "wings", it glides to a landing at the foot of the tree, then scrambles back up when it catches a glimpse of you. A tiny tree frog clings to the trunk, holding tight with the sticky pads on its toes.

Wherever you shine your light there's something else to see. Four Japanese beetles are asleep in a clump of goldenrod, their legs curled up under them. A slender green grasshopper clings to the top of a weed stalk, motionless in your light beam. Earthworms slither through the grass and a shiny slug glides up a flower stem. During the day when it hides under stones or boards, the slug is a fat, formless blob. At night, on the prowl for food, it's slender and graceful-looking with curious curving horns.

In a clump of grass a black and orange Garden Spider is making some repairs on her web. Her complicated structure, known as an orb web, is woven in a single night. When it is completed, the spider spins a silk "telephone" line from the center of the web to a nearby grass blade. Sitting on the grass holding the "telephone" line, she can feel the slightest vibration in the web. If you touch one of its strands as gently as you can, she'll scoot out of her hiding place to see who's calling.

Attracted by your light, a moth flies to the web. Quickly the spider pounces on the moth and wraps it in sticky silk. The moth bundle is scarcely completed when a Leafhopper blunders into the trap. After that a Lacewing, and then another moth. Thanks to your flashlight, the spider now has more business than she can handle. She runs frantically from one victim to the next, too busy to stop and enjoy the feast. By the time you leave, her beautiful web is torn and misshapen.

After you have gone she will suck her captives dry, then cut away the strands which hold them in the web. Days or weeks later, when she has had enough to eat, she

will lay her eggs, wrapping them carefully in a triple layer of silk. The newly hatched spiderlings are able to spin silk strands from the day of their birth.

Spiders have two legs too many to be classified with the insects—and at least four legs too many as far as most people are concerned! In spite of their appearance, they do a great deal more good than harm. Although most of them are too weak to bite through human skin, they are strong enough to kill vast quantities of flies and mosquitoes. And clever enough to spin a fine silk thread which is used in the manufacture of telescopes and gun sights.

## Forward March! Eyes Down!

No army officer would ever give a command like that, but if you want to know what's going on in the world of the night, it's well to keep your eyes on the ground. As soon as it grows dark, thousands of hunters leave their daytime hiding places. Flat-bodied, with long slender legs, they're built for running rather than flying. You'll seldom see these hunters at lights or on sugared trees because they prefer live meat. They are all members of one beetle family, the *Carabidae*, a name which means "cannibal."

They're also called Ground Beetles and Caterpillar Hunters. If you were to collect Ground Beetles from now until you are fifty, you'd never see all of them. In North America alone there are more than twenty-five hundred

GROUND BEETLES

different species, some no bigger than a fingernail and others larger than a thumb. Usually they're black or mahogany-brown, although one common Caterpillar Hunter has bright green wing covers.

They scoot through the grass, pouncing on caterpillars and slugs. Some Ground Beetles tear their victims to bits with their powerful jaws. Others paralyze them with a poisonous fluid. If you hold a piece of paper close to the head of one of the big Ground Beetles, you can watch it snip through the paper as if its jaws were scissors.

Even the Ground Beetle babies are cannibals. Hard-shelled, big-headed, they begin to hunt as soon as they're born. When a scientist followed a newly hatched larva, he found that it traveled almost two miles in a three-day period. Before it was full-grown, it had eaten fifty cater-pillars!

The busy beetles hide during the day under stones and in rotting logs. If you lift up a flat rock or a loose piece of bark, you'll probably see half a dozen of them scrambling for cover as soon as the light strikes them. In recent years shade trees in cities and suburbs have been badly infested with caterpillars of all kinds. That's because the trees are surrounded by smooth pavements and close-cropped lawns and there's no longer any place for the Caterpillar Hunters to hide.

## As Regular As Clockwork

It's interesting to bring a Ground Beetle home with you and watch how faithfully it sticks to its timetable. It will be quiet all day, hiding under any shelter you offer it. Then, just as your mother is preparing supper, it begins to scrabble around.

How does the beetle know when it's time to get up? Its movements don't seem to depend on light. It will awaken each evening whether you keep it under the brightest electric light or put it away in a dark windowless room.

Ground Beetles aren't the only insects who behave in this way. Fireflies kept in a jar will flash their lights for a short time at dusk and then wait twenty-four hours before flashing again. A captive moth, motionless all day, will begin to flutter its wings as soon as the sun goes down. Even though it can't see the sunset, even though you're shining a light on its cage, it will awaken and try to fly.

Almost all insects—butterflies as well as moths, bees as well as beetles—have built-in alarm clocks which tell them when to get up and when to sleep. These alarm clocks were set hundreds of thousands of years ago when insects were first developing. Originally, scientists think, the day insects were awakened by light and the night insects by the absence of light. Gradually, after the same behavior was repeated century after century, the timetables became automatic. Now, instead of depending on sunrise or sunset, each insect is aroused by its own built-in clock.

# Chapter Eight

## LISTEN!

On August and September evenings the insect orchestra is in full swing. Perhaps "orchestra" isn't quite the right word. The late-summer symphony sounds more like a kindergarten rhythm band where children blow on combs, toot whistles, and tap half-filled water glasses. No one keeps time with anybody else or attempts a tune, but everyone makes noise and has fun.

Sssh! Listen! What do you hear? Everywhere, coming at you from all sides, there's a swelling wave of sound. A buzzing, ticking, trilling ROAR fills your ears.

At first it's all one big noise. But if you stand very still and listen very hard, you can begin to sort it out. A tiny clock is ticking steadily in the grass. There's a buzz from the bushes, a tweet from the stone wall, and a conversational cackle in the branches over your head. All around, difficult to locate, is a musical, high-pitched trill.

As you move toward the music-makers, their sounds cease. It takes patience and the stealth of an Indian scout to track them down. Walk softly, pause, listen. When you're quiet, they'll start up again.

## First Fiddle

Now there's a steady chirp from a crack in the old stone wall and you can catch one of the musicians in your flashlight beam. He's a Field Cricket, a plump, shiny black creature with long threadlike antennae. His underwings are folded like a fan against his body, but his short upper wings are raised. As you watch, he moves them from side to side, rubbing them against each other. The wings move faster, faster, faster, until all you can see is a blur. Until all you can hear is an ear-piercing "TWE-E-E-T."

Each forewing has a rough round spot on its upper surface and a tiny toothed file underneath. When the cricket scrapes the rough spot over the file, his wings vibrate rapidly, as violin strings do when a bow is pulled across them. The faster he moves his wings, the higher pitched is the sound you hear.

The female cricket, usually larger than the male, has no musical instrument. All she can do is listen. She listens not with her antennae as most insects do, but with real honest-to-goodness ears. Real honest-to-goodness ears located on her front pair of legs just below her knees.

A scientist who wanted to be sure that she could hear with her legs tried an experiment. He put male and female crickets in separate cages. They weren't able to see each other, but their cages were connected by telephone. As soon as the males began to chirp, the females crowded around their receiver, listening attentively. When he removed their oddly placed ears, they made no movement at all, no matter how loudly the males fiddled.

Both male and female Field Crickets also have two pointed spikes at the tips of their abdomens. These spikes, which are covered with tiny hairs, pick up vibrations and help the insects find their way when they dart backward into their burrows. Alongside the spikes, female crickets have long pointed ovipositors which they use for digging holes in the ground and depositing their eggs.

Field Cricket eggs are usually laid late in summer. When the young hatch the next spring, they're tiny timid crea-

105

FIELD CRICKETS

tures who scurry away if you come near them. After half a dozen molts they develop square-cut amber-colored wings which darken as they grow older. Although they're expert jumpers, able to leap one hundred times the length of their bodies, they never fly.

As the Field Crickets begin to mate and lay eggs, they leave their separate underground burrows and look for company. Sometimes hundreds of them live side by side in a stone wall or under boards in a field. If you visit one of these cricket apartment houses in the daytime, you'll see inquisitive feelers and bright eyes poking out of every crevice. Scraps of bread scattered on the stone will often bring them outdoors. Even when they're eating they're watchful, however, and the slightest movement—a fluttering leaf, a flickering finger—will send them scrambling for shelter.

Every male Field Cricket knows two different songs, a courtship song which he addresses to a lady and a common, every-night song. Some scientists believe that this common

MALE FIELD CRICKETS

song is a warning to other males to keep away, some that it's only an expression of good feeling. Whatever you may think, when thousands of crickets sing together on a September evening they're LOUD. In more than one outdoor theater, actors have found it difficult to make themselves heard above the chirping crickets. They seem particularly noisy when the orchestra plays "Yankee Doodle!"

To many people, the chirping of a cricket sounds cheerful, suggesting the comforts of home and fireside. Perhaps you've heard of "The Cricket on the Hearth," a story by Charles Dickens in which a cricket brings good luck to a troubled household. Perhaps you'll even have a cricket on your own hearth next winter. Field crickets often come indoors in the fall to find a warm place in which to live.

FEMALE FIELD CRICKETS

One cricket on the hearth may bring good luck, but if too many come visiting, they're likely to be bothersome. Along with their close relatives, the roaches, they eat all sorts of things—including sweaters and woolen rugs—if they're hungry enough.

In many countries of Europe and Asia crickets have been kept in cages, like birds, so that people could listen to their songs. One particularly sweet-singing Oriental cricket, known as Golden Bell, was the favorite of Chinese emperors. The royal cricket chorus was housed in carved ivory and jade cages and fed cucumber slices and drops of honey from porcelain dishes.

Other Asian cricket fanciers raise the insects as fighters. The battling crickets are given special meals of rice and chestnuts with mosquitoes (fed on blood from their trainers' arms) for dessert. Before a fight, they are weighed in on tiny scales, just as boxers are here. If the fight is slow in getting under way, the trainers poke the insects with cricket ticklers made of rabbit whiskers fastened to bone handles. Soon the fighters leap at each other, kicking with their long hind legs and biting with their sharp jaws until one of the contestants is dead. Champion crickets have even been buried in small silver coffins!

It isn't necessary, of course, to keep crickets in ivory and jade cages. A mayonnaise jar or a flower pot with a lantern globe on top of it will do nicely. The crickets will eat kitchen scraps—lettuce, bread, apple slices, dog biscuit —and, occasionally, each other. At first they'll hide when you approach, but as they lose their shyness you'll be able to watch them feed and sing. Instead of burying them in silver coffins when they die, you can remove the wings of the males and rub them together to see what kind of music you can make.

*Believe-It-or-Not*

The big black Field Cricket is the most familiar cricket in the night band, but he's far from the only one. The steady ticking that you hear in the grass, the ticking that never seems to stop, is made by a smaller member of the Field Cricket family. Black-brown in color, he's less than half an inch long. What he lacks in size, he makes up for in persistence. Instead of chirping and pausing and chirping again, he fiddles continuously.

If there's a marshy meadow near your home, listen for a hoarse "Churr-Churr," almost a frog noise, that seems to come from under the ground. This solemn song is the song of a Mole Cricket. He's hard to find because he spends most of his life in an underground burrow, but once you've seen him you'll never forget him.

The Mole Cricket is a believe-it-or-not insect who doesn't look like other crickets or like anything else in the world but a mole. His broad front legs end in paws and he's covered with velvety, golden-brown fur. When he digs, his paws act as shovels, pushing the dirt aside with a breast-stroke motion.

MOLE CRICKETS

His burrow is a complicated apartment with tunnels connecting underground rooms. He lives there all year round, six inches below the surface, feeding on plant roots, worms, and insect larvae. Late in summer, during the mating season, he frequently comes out for a breath of fresh air. Sitting just inside the entrance of his tunnel, he rubs his forewings to produce his mournful sound. Sometimes he unfurls his long underwings and awkwardly flies to bright lights.

The female Mole Cricket looks very much like her mate. After laying a pile of eggs in an underground room which she has prepared, she stays in the nursery to protect her offspring from beetles—and from male Mole Crickets.

As soon as you put one of these funny-looking fellows in a jar with some dirt, it starts digging. It buries itself with incredible speed and once it's buried it doesn't reappear until evening. By looking along the sides and bottom of the jar, you may be able to watch it in its burrow.

ANGULAR-WINGED KATYDID

The insect who knows all and tells all about Katy is more often heard than seen. A member of the Long-horned Grasshopper family, he lives in the tops of trees. His bright green oval wings so closely resemble leaves that even if you climb up after him, you may not recognize him.

Not all Katydids sing about Katy. There's a different noise coming from the lower branches of a tree. It sounds as if someone was running his fingers over the teeth of a comb—or loudly winding a watch. As you poke among the leaves with your flashlight, you'll see a long-legged lettuce-green creature. Hanging head down, he's raising his wings in song.

There's nothing shy about this Angular-winged Katy-did. If you startle him, he's likely to spread his wings and head straight for you—until you're the one who is startled. He doesn't fly, but glides through the air the way a flying squirrel does. He can also put his powerful high-jumper legs to good use.

Late in summer the green, heart-shaped faces of Angular-winged Katydids often appear at your window. They're quite willing to be picked up and examined, although they may smear your fingers with brown "tobacco juice" saliva as grasshoppers do. Even without a magnifying glass you can see the ears on their front legs and the dark triangle at the base of the male's wings which he vibrates to make sounds.

The females have big curving ovipositors. They glue their eggs to the edges of leaves or in neat rows along a twig. In the South there are two Katydid broods each year, but in the North the eggs which are laid in fall don't hatch until the following spring. The newborn pale-green Katydids spend several months eating leaves before their wings appear.

Of all the creatures of the night, these Katydids are the most entertaining house guests. If there's a Japanese store in your town, try to buy a little wooden cricket cage to keep them in. They'll cling to the bars at the top of the cage, hanging upside down as if they were circus acrobats. Or they'll walk about slowly and deliberately, carefully lifting one gangling leg and then another. They feed on lettuce, taking tiny bites with their sidewise-moving jaws and solemnly cleaning themselves afterward. This all-over washing is comical to watch. Each foot is licked, each long antenna looped through the mouth many times a day.

Every once in a while one of the Katydids will escape from the cage. If he's a male, there's no need to hunt for him. Because when evening rolls around he'll announce his hiding place with a happy "Tzeet, Tzeet, Tzeet."

ANGULAR-WINGED KATYDIDS

## END OF STORY?

When you were little, all the stories that were read to you ended in the same way. "And everybody lived happily ever after." Because this is a true story, it has no ending.

One late October evening, you'll hear "Katy . . . Kate . . . Kay . . ." Like a mechanical toy that's in need of winding, the insect's wings are slowing down. The chirps grow fainter until there's nothing left but a hoarse buzz. After that, silence.

The summer songs are finished. The leaves have fallen from the trees. The grass in the fields is brown and there's a thin coat of ice on the pond. When you look out of your window you see white frost crystals instead of tapping feelers and fluttering wings.

Isn't this the end? Certainly not. There are Katydid eggs glued to the fallen leaves and fat white grubs curled up beneath the grass roots. There's a cocoon swinging from the bare branch of a tree and a shiny beetle resting under its bark. There's a row of Caddisfly houses on the muddy bottom of the pond and a colony of water bugs hiding among the weeds close to the shore.

On a warm night in March or April, the story will begin all over again.

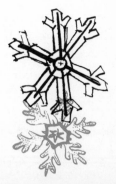

# MORE BOOKS

This book is only an introduction to the creatures of the night. It doesn't attempt to describe all of the insects that you will see this summer and next—after you really start looking for them. If you want to find out more about moths or beetles or bugs, the following books will be helpful.

*Field Book of Insects* by Frank E. Lutz, G. P. Putnam's Sons.

*Field Book of Ponds and Streams* by Ann H. Morgan, G. P. Putnam's Sons.

*Grassroot Jungles* by Edwin Way Teale, Dodd, Mead and Co.

*Insects* by Herbert S. Zim and Clarence Z. Cottam, Simon and Schuster.

*The Insect Book* by Leland O. Howard, Doubleday.

*The Insect Guide* by Ralph Swain, Doubleday.

*Insects: Their Secret World* by Evelyn Cheesman, William Sloane Associates.

*A Lot of Insects* by Frank E. Lutz, G. P. Putnam's Sons.

*The Moth Book* by W. J. Holland, Doubleday.

*Near Horizons* by Edwin Way Teale, Dodd, Mead and Co.

*The Wonderful World of Insects* by Albro Gaul, Rinehart and Co.